D1766167

MABEL
KEEPS CALM
AND
CARRIES ON

3 4114 00647 5247

MABEL KEEPS CALM AND CARRIES ON

THE WARTIME POSTCARDS OF

MABEL LUCIE ATTWELL

EDITED BY VICKI THOMAS

The History Press

BLACKPOOL LIBRARIES	
00647524	
Bertrams	17/06/2013
741.683	£9.99
	AN

First published 2013

The History Press
The Mill, Brimscombe Port
Stroud, Gloucestershire, GL5 2QG
www.thehistorypress.co.uk

© Text, Vicki Thomas, 2013
© Images, Lucie Attwell Ltd, 2013

The right of Vicki Thomas to be identified as the Author
of this work has been asserted in accordance with the
Copyrights, Designs and Patents Act 1988.

All rights reserved. No part of this book may be reprinted
or reproduced or utilised in any form or by any electronic,
mechanical or other means, now known or hereafter invented,
including photocopying and recording, or in any information
storage or retrieval system, without the permission in writing
from the Publishers.

British Library Cataloguing in Publication Data.
A catalogue record for this book is available from the British Library.

ISBN 978 0 7524 8919 3

Typesetting and origination by The History Press
Printed in India
Manufacturing managed by Jellyfish Solutions Ltd

CONTENTS

FOREWORD

My wife and I started Help for Heroes in 2007 as a charity to aid soldiers that were wounded in war, but I had to give up working full time as a cartoonist to fully devote my time to the charity. We have been delighted to feature some of Mabel Lucie Attwell's work on cards to raise funds for Help for Heroes as her approach to the hardships of war and rehabilitation embody the principles behind our work.

Mabel Lucie Attwell helped the heroes of the two world wars through her images and postcards; she wanted her work to raise people's spirits and help them to 'smile through the tears'. Even after facing tragedy at the death of her husband and son, as well as having to raise her family, she continued working on images that brought the nation hope, humour and spoke poignantly of their heartbreak.

My career as a cartoonist began when I was serving in the Royal Green Jackets. For me, war and the images I created were intertwined from the start, so I understand the importance of art in wartime. Such images give support for families, rally troops and send heartwarming messages to the front and back home. Mabel Lucie Attwell also understood the beneficial effect of a warm slogan and home comfort, especially in the hard times of war. She helped many

with her cheery postcards with cheeky captions offering an insight into the feelings and emotions of wartime. I think this really shows how amazing she was as a person, as an entrepreneur and as a woman. She was a relentless one-woman workforce and the greatness she achieved is illustrated perfectly by her wartime postcard work. The wartime images that fill these pages speak through the years and raise a smile today for young and old.

Bryn Parry
Co-founder of Help For Heroes
2013

ACKNOWLEDGEMENTS

Thanks are due to Andrew, William and Elizabeth Battle, John, Hilary and Mark Wickham of Lucie Attwell Ltd, John and Silvia Henty, Jo de Vries of The History Press, Georgia Standen, Rita and John Smith of Memories – Mabel Lucie Attwell Museum, Luci Gosling of Mary Evans Picture Library, Richard Dennis, the Imperial War Museum, the British Cartoon Archive at University of Kent, University of St Andrew's Library, the Design Research Group at University of Northampton and the design team at Vicki Thomas Associates. Thank you also to Bryn Parry of Help for Heroes for taking the time to write the foreword to the book, we are delighted to be supporting the charity with a donation from the sales going to Help for Heroes.

*****

Copyright in all the postcard images is the property of Lucie Attwell Ltd. All have been reproduced with their kind permission. Some of the images are no longer in their archive, so thanks are also due to John Henty, Richard Dennis, Rita and John Smith of Memories – Mabel Lucie Attwell Museum, Jo and Reg Richardson, and Vicki Thomas Associates for permission to reproduce postcards now in their collections.

INTRODUCTION

Mabel Lucie Attwell's highly successful career as a commercial artist spanned both the First and Second World Wars. The firms who commissioned her distinctive style were many and varied, but she built up a strong working relationship with the postcard publisher, Valentine's of Dundee. She illustrated books and greetings cards for British royalty, but most of her work was created to please and cheer everyone, whatever their status. Her popularity encouraged manufacturing companies and advertising agencies to commission her work to boost sales of everyday items such as Hovis bread and Dorma bed linen. The distinctive characters she created were produced as postcards, tableware, textiles, figurines and toys while her most famous characters, Bunty and the Boo-Boos, appeared in six books. This book is just a glimpse of a small part of her huge volume of work; the picture postcards she created in wartime, aimed at cheering those on the frontline and those struggling with the hardships of rationing and attacks on the Home Front.

Mabel Lucie was born in June 1879 to a large family and was the daughter of a successful butcher who ran several shops in the East End of London. Family life in the nineteenth century was traditional and by Mabel Lucie's own account her parents were not overtly affectionate.

Mabel Lucie
Attwell, *c*. 1920.

Despite their cold approach to parenting, her father encouraged dedication, practice and perfection, which resulted in several of her siblings also being artistic or musical and successful in later life.

It is noticeable in Mabel Lucie's early sketchbooks that her images reflect the need for comfort and the security of home. Her commercial images continued this theme and developed it for her audience, despite the changes occurring in her personal life and in the world around her.

Mabel Lucie started her artistic training at the London Guild-founded Coopers' Company Coborn School, where she was encouraged by her teacher to pursue her talents. She won her first commission by submitting work directly to one of the most successful card companies of the day, Raphael Tuck & Sons in 1902. This amazing connection allowed her to build up enough customers to fund herself through five years of art school, first at Heatherley's School of Fine Art and then St Martin's College of Art. However, Mabel Lucie did not complete the courses because she found that their formal approach conflicted with her own informal art style. One thing she did take away from her time at St Martin's College was her future husband, Harold C. Earnshaw, who, like Mabel Lucie, was already a successful illustrator working with book publishers like W.&R. Chambers, as well as Raphael Tuck & Sons. They married in 1908 with little fuss at a registry office and both artists took commissions away with them on honeymoon.

Pat, as Harold was known, was an active member of the Sketch Club, which included many prominent artists of the

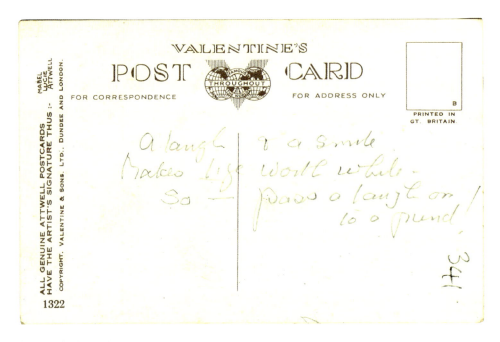

day, including the Heath Robinson brothers, Cecil Aldin and Tom Browne who were all providing commercial illustration to the growing advertising industry. However Mabel Lucie, despite being very much part of the artistic community in London, was not formally a member of the Sketch Club as women at the time were restricted from membership. Still, Mabel Lucie and Pat worked together, initially sharing studio space and some clients. His more formal artistic skills complemented hers and when required he was called on to use his talents to draw vehicles or more realistic animals. This help allowed Mabel Lucie the freedom to focus on her own unique talents and style.

This Valentine's card back is one from Mabel's studio collection and shows an alternative motto written in her own hand.

This Tuck card back illustrates how the cards were used to lift the spirits of those nearest and dearest to the sender. They continue to be traded by collectors and this one was re-sold for 50p at sometime in its past.

From 1908 she worked on a series of commissions from Raphael Tuck for gift books depicting fairy tales such as *Mother Goose's Nursery Rhymes*, *Grimm's and Hans Christian Andersen's Fairy Tales* and *Alice in Wonderland*. By 1914 she had completed twenty-two books for five major publishers. During the First World War she continued to work on books, including in 1915 an abridged version of Charles Kingsley's *The Water Babies*. Around the same time, Mabel Lucie began work on postcard designs. Some of her later designs featured characters from these books almost complaining about how their fantasy world has been disturbed by the outbreak of war.

In 1910 Pat and Lucie, as she signed her letters, set up home in Coulsdon, Surrey, which was only a short commute from London. They had two members of staff, which was not unusual before the war, including a nanny to look after their newly born daughter Peggy (also known as Marjorie). By the time of the 1911 census they are both listed as 'Painters (Artists)' working on their 'Own account' with two children, Peggy and the newborn Peter (Max). When her second son, Bill (Brian), was born in 1914, Mabel Lucie had found an artists' agency to represent her work. Francis & Mills, who boasted being 'Agents to the Best Artists', were dubious at first about taking on a woman but soon found her work sold well. It was to be the start of a long and beneficial working relationship.

She created some postcard designs before the First World War not only for Raphael Tuck & Sons but also Carlton, amongst others. In 1911 Valentine's of Dundee cautiously approached her to design postcards, cautiously as some artists preferred not to sell their work to postcard companies. Her signature style developed quite quickly, in her own words from an interview in 1914:

> My idea is not so much to draw children for children, as to introduce them, if I may put it so, with all their lovable and comical ways to the grown-ups.

In 1914 she had three young children of her own and they must have inspired her. One or two of the early illustrations look like her daughter, Peggy, but her sons report when asked that they did not generally pose for her, as she says it was their 'ways' that she captured.

She went on in a later newspaper article to describe her audience and unique approach:

I draw mainly for adults: for the suburbanite, the mother, the demi-mondaine, the country gossip, the cockney housewife, the young married couple, the shopgirl, the flapper, the faithful wife and the unfaithful, the 'grown-up' and the not so good. I see the child in the adult, then I draw the adult as a child. The situation, the stance and the vocabulary are taken from children, but the message is between adults – me and any other. Children would not understand that message.

The series of postcards included in this book clearly show the development of this approach. Nevertheless that view does not stop children of all ages enjoying her work. Chad Valley Dolls approached her to design a range of dolls based on her characters and the dolls are often seen as companions in the images. Valentine's in-house journal reports that her images made it to the Western Front and were found decorating a trench, which was lost and regained by the Allies, and that the prints were appreciated by all the residents.

In 1915 Pat enlisted in the Artists' Rifles, as the name implies it was made up of painters, sculptors and architects. He was sent to the Somme and was involved in patrols of a light railway supplying the frontline. In 1916 Pat was injured by a shell explosion and lost his right arm. This tragedy brought home the reality of war for Mabel Lucie. Pat had to re-learn to draw with his left hand and while he recovered she had to work hard to support the whole family.

In the inter-war period her relationship with her clients and the public expanded. Pathé and Gaumont both filmed her for their newsreels in cinemas. Famously, J.M. Barrie asked her to illustrate a gift book version of *Peter Pan*. She also collaborated with the Queen of Romania on two fairy tale books, travelling to Romania at her invitation. In contrast to the postcards, Mabel Lucie started to produce a yearly annual whose illustrations and stories were primarily for children to enjoy.

On top of this, Mabel Lucie's relationship with Valentine's grew and she was their bestselling artist. They started to produce other products: books, calendars, greeting cards and stationery. It was with them that she began to develop her own characters, Bunty and the Boo-Boos, in 1913. By 1926, the book illustrations were being reprinted as postcards and were reproduced in ceramics by Shelley Potteries.

This photograph of Mabel Lucie in her studio with her son Brian and artwork for postcards in the background, in the 1920s, gives a good idea of how she worked. The originals were painted larger than their print size and reduced for printing. She worked mainly in watercolour, usually Winsor and Newton, but unusually used white paint on white board. The postcard publishers encouraged her to use more colour in her backgrounds, so the cards did not

Mabel Lucie at work, with her son Brian.

become so easily shop soiled. Over the years, gouache paint was also used to create larger areas of solid colour that were easier to print. Bands and borders of red and yellow appear and later blue and black backgrounds to suit the design. Her grandsons distinctly remember a large pot of blue paint in her studio in Cornwall.

This is the era of the humorous postcard as well as the pictorial view. Valentine's had other artists like Mabel's husband Pat, and George Studdy with Bonzo the Dog. No history of these decades should ignore Donald McGill's postcards for their saucy nature embodies key aspects of the British sense of humour. Elfreda Buckland, McGill's biographer, calculates that around 800 million picture postcards were sent in 1914. Mabel Lucie's postcard royalty payments indicate that sales remained good over the fifty years of her collaboration with Valentine's.

The Valentine's postcard collection grew by twenty-four images a year. Mabel Lucie wrote many of the captions herself but also accepted feedback from her agents and publishers. Some of the correspondence survives and provides a good insight into her close working relationship with the publisher. Mabel and Pat bought a studio flat in London so they could keep in touch with their professional contacts; she became an active member of Chelsea Arts Club and was elected to the Society of Women Artists. In 1925 after various family homes in the country, they moved the family back to London. After finding a town house in South Kensington the family moved again in the 1930s. She was to continue to have a foothold in both town and country during the Second World War.

The 1930s brought economic depression for many and for the Earnshaw family it brought personal sorrow. Their son Peter had a car crash and took time to recover, and his sibling Brian did not survive pneumonia in 1935. However more grief was to come when Pat passed away in 1937. Mabel Lucie continued to work despite what must have been great sadness. The ability to have her characters cry and continue to 'smile through the tears' may have helped her cope, but also in her grief she created images that others

could use to communicate sympathy. These images were particularly suited to Britain as country of the 'stiff upper lip' where traditionally people struggled to express sympathy or grief; Mabel Lucie's images with their unique blend of humour and poignancy were to prove invaluable in allowing them to do so.

On the eve of war in 1939, Mabel Lucie moved into a new house in Victoria Road, London but she also had a separate studio space by the Thames, away from the family home. To assist with her move Valentine's printed a change of address card exclusively for Mabel Lucie with her address on the back and the design was later reprinted as a postcard.

When asked in 1961 about her wartime experience for an interview in *Modern Woman* magazine she replied:

> During the Second World War, I worked alone in an empty building by the Thames. It had been used by the Thames Conservancy Board. When the war came, they moved out and I was moved in. I stayed there for most of the war. I never went down into an air raid shelter. I was too busy trying to make people laugh about wartime bread and sausages, instead of crying about them.

Her studio may have survived bombs, but a landmine damaged her house in Victoria Road and she was forced to stay in the Norfolk Hotel near her agent's office for some months. Regular correspondence survives from clients and her agent from 1939–41 indicating that she made frequent visits to her daughter's home Froxfield, near Marlborough.

Peggy's marriage had not been an ideal one and with a young family, her mother's support must have been important.

The bombing of London destroyed much of the East End where Mabel Lucie was born, but it also destroyed Raphael Tuck & Sons' office in Moorfields on 29 December 1940, and along with the building much of the original artwork she and many other artists had created for books and cards. It was hard for the firm to rebuild their business after this catastrophe.

In 1945 Mabel Lucie received a letter from Pathé Pictures asking to interview her for 'our popular magazine *The New Pathé Pictorial*'. Also during this period, requests to work with Walt Disney were flattering but rebuffed as she felt her characters were British and that they would need to be changed too much for an American audience.

A new London home was found in Aubrey Hill W8, where she was based until she moved to Fowey in Cornwall permanently in 1946. There seem to be various reasons for the move; she had family connections to the town, it provided a retreat and the artistic circle she favoured had communities in St Ives and Dartington in the inter-war period. The house itself was chosen because it had a telephone, so she could keep in contact with her family and business associates. She may have been sixty-five but it was far from a retirement. It was to be the registered address for her company Lucie Attwell Ltd and her son Peter moved with her and acted as her assistant.

She continued to work and in the 1950s her daughter Peggy Wickham stepped into help with the postcard designs and collaboration with Valentine's. They carried on the tradition but do not have the same appeal to the public, as those her mother created in the decades when she had reason to make us all smile.

Bright-eyed and reflecting on her life in 1964, she commented:

> My life has been good and sad. I have, according to many letters I have received, given a lot of happiness to a lot of people through two world wars.

She was an extraordinary woman, speaking to everyone through her paintings and allowing them to communicate with loved ones in a very personal and distinctive way. When asked in 1961, what was her greatest achievement, for an article in *Modern Woman Magazine*, she replied:

> My marriage – no, my first baby. Achievement is the wrong word. But yes, motherhood was the most wonderful thing in my life. My career is me and my pictures are me, but no artist, writer or scientist, could make anything as perfect as a baby, and yet through me, it had been done. I couldn't believe it.

Through these postcards we can see what was also important to her. Many of the images seem to be her and her response to the times in which she lived. She underplays her role in the war years but she certainly lifted the nation's spirit.

THE FIRST WORLD WAR

The First World War saw a proliferation of postcards and silks published, often displaying patriotic messages that were sent from Britain to the Western Front and Mabel's postcards were produced in thousands, even finding their way into the trenches.

Your King & Country Need You

In August 1914 with the outbreak of war, there was a desperate need to recruit more men into the British Army. The famous posters 'Your King & Country Need You' were issued as part of a propaganda drive that saw 33,000 men joining up every day for the first few weeks. A few of the postcards from the early days of the war seem to echo the feeling that everyone had to enlist and not bear the disgrace of receiving a white feather, given out by women to those men deemed to be cowards for not serving on the frontline. At first sight, Mabel Lucie's character does not seem happy about the call to arms, although the caption tells a different and far more patriotic story.

Your King & Country Need You
Alfred Stiebel & Co.
*c.*1914

Return of the Hero

This postcard is considered by many collectors to be a 'portrait' of Mabel Lucie Attwell and her husband Harold Earnshaw upon his return from serving with the Artists' Rifles. He was injured by shrapnel in his right arm and had to learn to draw with his left hand in order to continue his artistic career. He was certainly a hero in her eyes and those of the artistic community. He later commented: 'I don't think I felt sorry for myself, but I remember thinking "pity it wasn't my left".'

Return of the Hero
The Carlton Publishing Co.
*c.*1914

Return of the hero.

A Woman's Duty

The Salute

'Return of the Hero' was one of a series of cards published by Carlton, five of which feature women during wartime. Three postcards feature girls dressed as Red Cross nurses taking care of toy 'soldiers', the others depict women's work in caring for their children whilst their father is away, or knitting warm garments for their loved ones at the front. The nurse Edith Cavell took her welfare responsibilities further and aided soldiers caught behind enemy lines in Belgium to return home and she was executed as a spy for her actions. The soldier's salute, in the illustration could be for the nurse rather than the 'wounded soldier'.

The Red Cross was founded in 1863, creating a neutral, impartial help for the wounded and sick in wars. Many women during the First World War volunteered to work as nurses and many ended up working close to the frontlines. Mabel Lucie continued to support the organisation and at the beginning of the Second World War she was asked contribute an illustration entitled 'The Evacuee' to a book. The book was sold to raise money for the Red Cross, and she was among other contributors including Rex Whistler, Ivor Novello, Laura Knight, Frank Brangwyn and Edmund Dulac, indicating her status at the time.

A Woman's Duty
The Carlton
Publishing Co.
*c.*1914

The Salute
The Carlton
Publishing Co.
*c.*1915

A woman's duty.

The Salute.

All the Girls Love a Sailor

Under Fire

These two postcards have layouts that Mabel Lucie would return to later in her career. They show her humour and the tongue-in-cheek captions that are typical of her. Clearly she drew inspiration from a popular song of the day 'All the Girls Love a Sailor' by A.J. Mill & B. Scott which came from a show called 'Ship Ahoy' (1909).

All the Girls Love a Sailor
The Carlton
Publishing Co.
*c.*1914

Under Fire
The Carlton
Publishing Co.
*c.*1914

"All the nice girls love a Sailor."

Les marins sont en vogue

"Under Fire."

The War Baby

Mabel Lucie said 'she sees the child in the adult and draws the adult as a child'. This image clearly shows that view of the world, with the almost naked babe smoking and standing to attention. Harold Earnshaw was a smoker so this may represent the child she saw in him. Many of the soldiers who went to war were very young and all were someone's child, many were to become known as the Doomed Youth or Lost Generation immortalised after the war in poetry, art and film. Mabel's later images are more child-like and no others feature smoking.

The War Baby
Raphael Tuck & Sons
*c.*1915

Eyes right !

THE WAR BABY
(Undress Uniform)

U-Nasty Boat!

This card image is very similar to an illustration for *The Water Babies* that she was working on at the same time for Raphael Tuck & Sons. German U-boats were deployed from the beginning of the war sinking British cruisers and merchant shipping, but they also suffered losses and were not fully committed against the Allies until towards the end of the war. The British press reported heavily on the U-boat war and public opinion against this seemingly 'invisible enemy' was very strong. It was also in 1915 that a U-boat hit the RMS *Lusitania*, which sank claiming the lives of its 1,198 passengers. It was this event that has often been seen as one of the major catalysts for bringing America into the war.

U-Nasty Boat!
Raphael Tuck & Sons
*c.*1915

Have You Seen Any Germans?

Valentine's also commissioned Mabel Lucie to work on cards with a seaside theme, but the wartime ones were produced in black and white, like this one. This image was later reworked in full colour with a different caption 'Who's little brudder are oo?' The postcard perhaps alludes to the preoccupation that the British had with an invasion from Germany by sea during the war.

Have You Seen Any Germans?
Valentine's
*c.*1915

What is the Good of a New Hat?

The Very Image of Daddy

Mabel Lucie was also undertaking commissions from magazines like *The Tatler* and *The Daily Sketch*. She uses a similar caption and layout for a cover design reproduced in black and white. Expensive fashions were no longer seen as appropriate in wartime. Many of Mabel's characters replace hats with bows and coloured bows with black versions. Bunty, the little girl in her Boo-Boo books seems to wear her black bow with pride well into the next decade and a father-type figure who carries her home in one story is dressed in khaki. Women during the war would often not see their husbands for very long periods of time, interspersed with brief periods of leave, many men would return home to meet for the first time a baby son or daughter that had been conceived either before they joined up or when they were on leave, these new arrivals could at first come as a bit of a shock!

What is the Good of a New Hat?
Valentine's (4205)
1916

The Very Image of Daddy
Valentine's (4207)
1916

WHAT IS THE GOOD OF A NEW HAT
WHEN TOMMY IS AWAY AT THE WAR?

THE VERY IMAGE OF DADDY!

More Zepps Coming Over

There were fifty-two Zeppelin airship bombing raids in Britain starting in 1915, including some in Purley, South London not far from the Earnshaws' home. These were attacks not against soldiers but civilians causing around 500 casualties during the war. The East of London where Mabel Lucie was brought up was deeply affected. With no purpose-built shelters and their silent attack, the lights went out all over the city and people went to bed, leaving only searchlights hunting the night skies. This was later reprinted as 'Goodnightie! Pleasant Dreams', this may be a play on the words of the popular wartime song 'Good-bye-ee', composed by R.P. Weston and Bert Lee in 1915.

More Zepps Coming Over
Valentine's (4209)
1916

MORE 'ZEPPS' COMING OVER—I MUST
PUT ON MY LOVELY NEW NIGHTIE!

All for the Love of a Soldier

The women left at home were missing their loved ones and looking forward to the future. Knitting for those serving in the forces and taking care of children feature in Mabel Lucie's artwork, but women are also seen preparing themselves for their partner's safe return home. Mabel's cards are full of references to changing fashion and the attempts made by housewives to look good with limited resources.

All for the Love of a Soldier
Valentine's (4012)
1916

ALL FOR THE LOVE OF A SOLDIER.

My Only Comfort

Tommy Comes Home on Leave

---

*My Only Comfort
While You Are Away*
Valentine's (4208)
1916

*Tommy Comes Home
on Leave*
Valentine's (4210)
1916

MY ONLY COMFORT
WHILE YOU ARE AWAY!

TOMMY COMES HOME ON LEAVE
TO-MORROW!

I'll Cut You Off

The Boy who Exceeded

War brings shortages and rationing and Mabel Lucie's characters are encouraged to play their part. Mabel Lucie in her turn recycled and reused her images changing the caption once the war was over and republishing them in the early 1920s. The scissors design was first published with the motto 'War Economy: Where is Daddy's best coat? I want to make a kettle holder!' Children do not lift hot kettles and they were not imprisoned for eating too much; these are images of adults drawn as their inner children, as such they are a poignant reminder of the hardships of war for both children and adults alike.

I'll Cut You Off
Valentine's (4306)
1916

The Boy who Exceeded
Valentine's (4424)
1917

I'LL CUT YOU OFF
        MY LIST OF FRIENDS
IF YOU DON'T WRITE ME SOON.

THE BOY WHO EXCEEDED HIS
FOOD RATIONS.

Put Out That Light!

This is an odd one out, as it is the only one of this set that has a painted background reminiscent of her *Water Babies* illustrations in layout and colouring. The humour of this warden demanding the sun to set makes light of a serious official campaign asking the public to observe the blackout, which was intended to make it harder for the enemy to find their targets.

Put Out That Light!
Valentine's (4305)
1916

"PUT OUT THAT LIGHT"

Who's Afraid of the Dark?

We's Not Afraid of the Dark

Mabel Lucie's characters are not afraid of the blackout or anything else. These cards may seem racist but the first ranges she created for Valentine's were multicultural, if stereotypes, for her day and feature not only African but also Japanese, Native American and Dutch children. They reflect the time of empires and the extent of British influence internationally. Soldiers were coming from across the world to fight for the Crown. In fact Mabel's cards were translated and exported widely, as seen by the French translation on the earlier sailor design.

Who's Afraid of the Dark?
Valentine's (4422)
1917

We's Not Afraid of the Dark
Valentine's (4417)
1917

WHO'S AFRAID OF THE DARK?

WE'S NOT AFRAID OF THE DARK.

A Sign of Peace

A Problem in Reconstruction

The soldier returns and looks like he has grown out of his suit clothes but carries a bouquet for the lass he left at home. Rebuilding after the war would not prove swift and people would have to make do for some time to come, but they were ready to enjoy themselves.

A Sign of Peace
Valentine's (4425)
1917

A Problem in Reconstruction
Valentine's (4691)
1918

A SIGN OF PEACE.

A PROBLEM IN RECONSTRUCTION.

I Hope They are Not Referring to Me

Mabel Lucie's character with her enormous black pom-pom thinks 'I hope they are not referring to me' on seeing the newspaper headlines in 1923. So many women were widowed or would never have the opportunity to marry because of all the losses. The First World War had seen women dominate the workplace for the first time and yet they were expected to return back to their pre-war domestic roles once the men came home. This was a period when women's rights, particularly embodied by the Suffragette Movement, were coming to the fore. However, her later pictures show that they were far from superfluous to the country's needs in the Second World War.

I Hope They are Not Referring to Me
Valentine's (749)
1923

THE SECOND WORLD WAR

The year that the Second World War broke out saw Mabel Lucie moving home and the war years were to see future moves. However, Mabel Lucie was determined that the war would not stop her work and she paid little heed to air-raid warnings, continuing to paint and create her humorous postcards, aimed at cheering the nation and reflecting the need to 'keep calm and carry on', 'make do and mend', 'dig for victory', as well as remembering to 'smile through the tears'.

Notice of Removal

This design was created for her own removal to a new home in West London, and was also made available as part of the Valentine's range. If the girls in her cards are her alter ego, then maybe the slightly bemused lonely figure on the tailboard is Mabel Lucie herself in 1939.

These are Certainly Moving Times

Mabel Lucie moved her London home several times during the war. Her son Peter enjoyed playing popular songs and this seems to refer to the famous words for 'My Old Man', as she follows the van on foot carrying the fireside furniture, an aspidistra in a pot and 'cock linnet'. This card has an extra quotation on the back:

This is a time for everyone to stand together, and hold firm!

The Prime Minister

Notice of Removal
Valentine's (2479)
1939

These are Certainly Moving Times
Valentine's (607)
1942

Here is the News

Mabel Lucie Attwell read several newspapers regularly and admired Churchill's leadership.

Here is the News
Valentine's (605)
1942

HERE IS THE NEWS—
AN' IT'S *ME* READING IT!

BRITAIN GOES TO WAR

England Expects

As at the outbreak of the First World War, in 1939 there was a great pressure on men to join-up once war was declared.

England Expects
Valentine's (4188)
1938

ENGLAND EXPECTS ——!

Good-bye!

By the end of 1939 1.5 million people had been conscripted into the British forces. The Second World War was to see in total nearly 6 million British personnel deployed all over the world in a variety of roles.

Good-bye!
Valentine's (183A)
1939

GOOD-BYE!—IF IT BE
FOR A YEAR—OR A DAY.
WE'LL BE LOVIN' YOU STILL—
IN THE SAME OLE WAY!

MABEL
LUCIE
ATTWELL

You Can Get a Bit of Peace

in the Army!

Johnny Get your Gun

You Can Get a Bit of Peace in the Army!
Valentine's (209)
1939

Johnny Get your Gun
Valentine's (4748)
1939

JOHNNY GET YOUR GUN!

Oo these Uniforms Get Me!

Mabel Lucie was not the only one moving and saying good-bye and 'wiping a tear from the eye-ee'. All over the country people were saying 'cheerio' to their loved ones, not knowing when or if they would return. Despite this, Mabel Lucie's images put a positive spin on being in the forces; having experienced the First World War, people generally had a better idea what war might mean and were more prepared for it, although the sheer scale of the war and the attacks on the Home Front were to change the lives of millions.

Oo these Uniforms Get Me!
Valentine's (A270)
1939

Oo! THESE UNIFORMS GET ME!

Be Good 'Til I/You Comes Back

I'd Likes to be Your 'Truly Friend'

There are not many images of soldiers in uniform on Mabel Lucie's Second World War postcards. Perhaps he is asking to be her pen pal; letters from home were vital to keeping up morale. The postcard was cheap and simple to send and the images could speak louder than words and help people to express their sentiments. In fact some cards were cheaper to send if you limited it to five words, hence the popularity of phrases like 'Wish you were here' with just your signature added for a personal touch. Such brief postcards were often the only way for couples to keep in touch. Serving soldiers could not say much about their deployment so the images had to speak for them.

Be Good 'Til I/You Comes Back
Valentine's (4750)
1939

I'd Likes to be Your 'Truly Friend'
Valentine's (211)
1939

BE GOOD——TIL' $\frac{I}{YOU}$ COMES BACK !

I'D LIKES TO BE YOUR "TRULY FRIEND."

Sure – We Can Squeeze You in

Somewhere!

At the beginning of the war the government encouraged children to move away from large cities that were likely to be bombed. Several of Mabel Lucie's cards were adapted to be used by evacuees to help them to communicate with home and to offer reassurance that they were safe and not forgotten.

Sure – We Can Squeeze You in Somewhere! Valentine's (212) 1939

HERE'S A SMILE AND A JOLLY P.C.
TO MY OWN LITTLE
LOVING EVACUEE.

DEAR MUMS I'SE HAPPY.
THAT'S ALL TO-DAY
CAN'T THINK OF ANYTHING MORE TO SAY.
YOUR LOVING EVACUEE.

Hullo Children Everywhere

Princesses Elizabeth and Margaret made a radio broadcast appearing on Uncle Mac's children's programme to offer their sympathies to evacuated children. The caption for one of her cards is based on the programme's catchphrase – 'Hullo, Children Everywhere'. It features two children, possibly even the young princesses. Princess Margaret was certainly a collector of Mabel Lucie's work and the palace commissioned Mabel Lucie to illustrate a Christmas card for her in 1940.

In the era before television was in everyone's homes, radio was important for the news and entertainment, and the wireless is illustrated on several cards.

Hullo Children Everywhere
Valentine's (398)
1940

HULLO CHILDREN—EVERYWHERE.

Happy Landings

The Royal Air Force had played a key role in the defence of the country during the Battle of Britain and Mabel Lucie acknowledges their efforts with a more specific design, for some possibly too toy-like and playful.

Happy Landings
Valentine's (716)
1943

H APPY

LANDINGS !

Hopes You Know We Love You So!

Women also worked in building and servicing planes and some flew, delivering aircraft ready for combat. The little girl in 'Hopes You Know We Love You So', who is dressed in patriotic red, white and blue and sports a sweetheart brooch given to her by one of the crew flying high above, caught the mood better.

Hopes You Know We Love You So!
Valentine's (715)
1943

Every Nice Boy Loves a Sailor

Valentine's wrote to Mabel Lucie in October 1941:

> Congratulations on the wholehearted support of the
> Powers that Be at the Admiralty and their sanction to the
> use as a Christmas card of 'Every Nice Boy Loves a Sailor'.
> We don't, of course, want their order, especially, as late as
> this but we are meeting them as a compliment to you.

1941 was the year Christmas card printing was banned; so
using a postcard instead was a way around the restrictions.

One of the arguments for not allowing women in the navy
in earlier generations is that they wore skirts and they would
have to climb ladders that would not have been seemly.
So Mabel Lucie has created a very positive image for those
serving in the 1940s, creating a new variant on the lyrics
from a First World War song.

*Every Nice Boy Loves
a Sailor*
Valentine's (678)
1942

"Every nice boy loves a sailor"

You Know *What Men Are!*

W.A.T.S. Doing?

Her agent suggested girls in uniform of different services in April 1941, he put forward, 'I'm doing my bit' or 'There is nothing I cannot tackle' as a caption but Mabel Lucie was more playful in her choice. They also produced a postcard of a single girl in khaki uniform and leather gloves, with the motto 'W.A.T.S doing?'. The letters stand for Women's Auxiliary Territorial Units (ATS), the gloves are for driving; the unit's most famous member was Princess Elizabeth.

You Know What Men Are!
Valentine's (706)
1943

W.A.T.S. Doing?
Valentine's (4749)
1939

"YOU KNOW WHAT MEN ARE!"

W.A.T'S DOING?

4749

Nuffing! I'll Get Along Alright!

Wot a War!!

The Royal Army Service Corps (RASC) was the part of the
British Army responsible for transports and the supply of
food, water, fuel and general requirements such as clothing,
furniture and stationery to offices and barracks. Many
women working in the forces during the war were involved
in keeping offices and barracks running smoothly. Mabel
Lucie developed her own 'method' of making sure her houses
ran smoothly. In this image the character has charmed a lift
from the army, thus saving on the petrol ration.

Nuffing! I'll Get Along Alright!
Valentine's (214)
1939

Wot a War!!
Valentine's (737)
1943

PETROL RATIONS—NUFFING! I'LL GET ALONG ALL RIGHT!

WOT A WAR!!
YES—IT'S A FINE JOB OF WORK
I'VE GOT—BUT I MANAGE TO THINKS
OF YOU—QUITE A LOT!

I'se Being a Good Little Girl!

Mabel Lucie's illustrations are often humorous, but many also draw out the poignancy of loss and the emptiness experienced by those left behind on the Home Front.

I'se Being a Good Little Girl!
Valentine's (399)
1940

"I'SE BEING A GOOD LITTLE GIRL!"

Got Any 'Leave' Left?

OO When I Think of You

Once you wave goodbye, you look forward to their return. Several of Mabel Lucie's designs are a little saucy with her characters promising hugs and kisses on the serviceman's return or reassuring their lovers of their fidelity. Members of the armed services were granted leave from time to time but only a few days and people tried to make them special days.

Got Any 'Leave' Left?
Valentine's (753)
1944

OO When I Think of You
Valentine's (4427)
1939

GOT ANY 'LEAVE' LEFT?

Oo! WHEN I THINKS ABOUT YOU!

I've Gone Crackers

It's Nice to be in Civvies Again

I've Gone Crackers
Valentine's (133)
1939

It's Nice to be in Civvies Again
Valentine's (391)
1940

Several of these designs were created with feedback from her agents and Valentine's requested a pink border to 'I've Gone Crackers' and seaside images but with a wartime twist.

I'VE GONE CRACKERS
OVER A SOLDIER.

IT'S NICE TO BE IN "CIVIES"
AGAIN FOR A BIT!

MAKING DO AND MENDING

Darling Mine I'm Feeling Fine

Many postcards were sent to the frontline to reassure loved ones that those back home were coping, as troops read about the deprivations of rationing and air raid attacks were naturally concerned for their friends and family.

Darling Mine I'm Feeling Fine
Valentine's (395)
1940

DEAR DARLIN' MINE—
I'M FEELIN' FINE!

When Fuel Restrictions are in the Bin

Fuel rationing also affected the amount of hot water one could use, so a deep bath was a luxury. Mabel Lucie's most famous product is her bath plaque published first in 1927 by Valentine's. She produced variants with different images and new verses. In wartime people were away from home and had to share bathrooms with strangers and these plaques were found in lodgings and guests houses nationwide. They are still in production, warning us:

Please remember – don't forget!
Never leave the bathroom wet.
Nor leave the soap still in the water–
That's a thing you <u>never</u> ought'er!–
And as you've been so often told.
<u>Never</u> let the 'hot' run 'cold':
Nor leave the towels upon the floor.
Nor keep the bath an hour or more–
When other folks are wanting one;
Just don't forget –<u>it isn't</u> done!–
An' if you'd really do the thing–
There's not the slightest need to sing!

Some of her postwar clients had wartime connections, for example, her illustrations were used on soaps produced by British Legion Industries for many years, giving employment and generating income for veterans and their families.

When Fuel Restrictions are in the Bin
Valentine's (825)
1945

We's Doing our Bit

I'm Doin' me Knit

Knitting for soldiers, was a task for those who stayed at home, women (titled or not) and children alike. Helmet hats or balaclavas made tin helmets more comfortable and could be pulled down when conditions were cold and wet. Knitting was promoted on both sides of the conflict and throughout the Commonwealth.

We's Doing our Bit
Valentine's (2246)
1932 reprinted

I'm Doin' me Knit
Valentine's (210)
1939

WHO'S WOOL-GATHERING NOW?

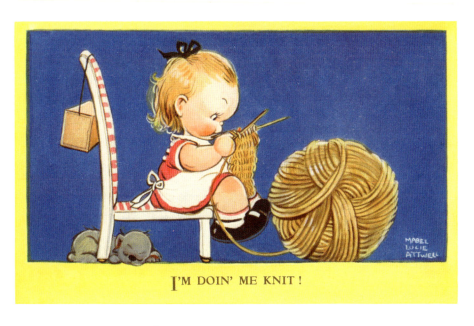

I'M DOIN' ME KNIT!

Portrait of an English Lady

Never Saying Die!

Wool without Coupons

Mabel Lucie's characters are seen to be struggling to produce socks and sweaters using wool in appropriate shades. The Red Cross provided instructions in the book that Mabel Lucie contributed to in 1939.

Portrait of an English Lady Never Saying Die!
Valentine's (494)
1940

Wool without Coupons
Valentine's (719)
1943

PORTRAIT OF AN ENGLISH LADY NEVER SAYING DIE!

"WOOL WITHOUT COUPONS!"

We have no Coupons...

Wool without Coupons Girls –

Everybody's Doing It

There are also several images of knitted clothing being unravelled. Often old jumpers were reknitted into squares and then stitched to make colourful blankets.

Worn adult jumpers would provide wool for a new child's cardigan. The tradition of women giving knitted garments to family members continues in British culture and humour with jokes being made about receiving too many socks or creatively knitted jumpers from aunts at Christmas each year. Knitting for soldiers and refugees still continues today. Taking up needles and wool for others in need started well before 1914, but Mabel focussed on the fun, love and comfort it provided.

We have no Coupons...
Valentine's (508)
1933 designed

Wool without Coupons Girls –
Everybody's Doing It
Valentine's (613)
*c.*1940

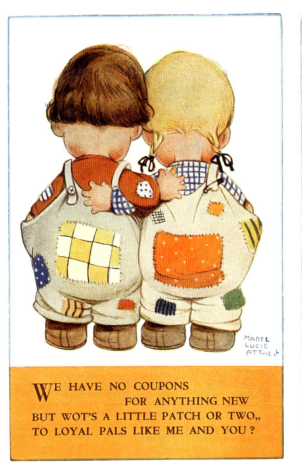

WE HAVE NO COUPONS
        FOR ANYTHING NEW
BUT WOT'S A LITTLE PATCH OR TWO,,
TO LOYAL PALS LIKE ME AND YOU?

WOOL WITHOUT COUPONS GIRLS—
EVERYBODY'S DOIN' IT NOW!

Anyone Seen me Coupons

'Make do and mend' was a necessity, as well as a government campaign during the war. Clothes were rationed and some items were scarce so one had to make do and adapt what you had. Mabel Lucie certainly saw the funny side of it; clothes are too small, others too large when they are passed on, household fabrics are turned into frocks and worn clothes into patches for quilts and mending. Nothing was wasted and some restrictions lasted into the 1950s.

Must Have a Nice New Suit

Somehow!

Anyone Seen me Coupons
Valentine's (603)
1942

Must Have a Nice New Suit Somehow!
Valentine's (704)
1943

ANY ONE SEEN ME COUPONS!

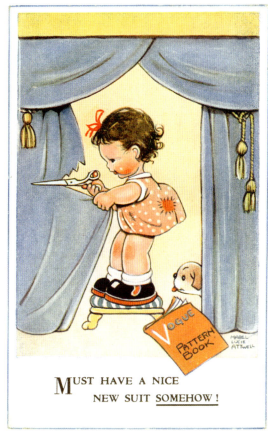

MUST HAVE A NICE
NEW SUIT SOMEHOW!

Now Can I Cover my Toes

or Blow my Nose?

Now Can I Cover
my Toes or Blow my
Nose?
Valentine's (606)
1942

Can't Have a Tablecloth and a Shirt

Can't have a
Tablecloth and a Shirt
Valentine's (755)
1944

NOW—CAN I COVER MY TOES—OR BLOW MY NOSE?

"CAN'T HAVE A TABLECLOTH AND A SHIRT!"

Muvvers Got no Drawing Room Rug

Muvvers Got no
Drawing Room Rug
Valentine's (535)
1941

Visible Mending

Visible Mending
Valentine's (820)
1945

"MUVVER'S GOT NO DRAWING ROOM HEARTH-RUG NOW!"

 ISIBLE MENDING – THAT'S ME!

DIGGING FOR VICTORY

England – My England!

'England, My England' is the title of poem written by
William Ernest Henley. Mabel Lucie drew on the wealth of
English literature for her captions. Poetry was also used on
the back of the cards in the war years:

Not once or twice in our roughs island story
The path of duty was the way to glory.

Tennyson

*England – My
England!*
Valentine's (489)
1940

MABEL
LUCIE
ATTWELL

ENGLAND—MY ENGLAND!

I'm Full of Health

This image seems to portray a 'land girl', working to provide food when extra hands were needed on the farm. The layout echoes some of the propaganda posters produced in the decade, showing factory workers with planes rather than birds flying over. Women volunteered to replace working men in all sorts of occupations, freeing them for military service.

I'm Full of Health
Valentine's (611)
1942

I'M FULL OF HEALTH—
HOW'S YOURSELF!

Just Wondering How You are Getting On!

Hopes to See Whole Lots of You Soon

Just Wondering How
You are Getting On!
Valentine's (397)
1940

Hopes to See Whole
Lots of You Soon
Valentine's (564)
1941

JUS' WONDERING HOW'S YOU ARE GETTING ON!

HOPES TO SEE
WHOLE LOTS
OF YOU SOON

It Will be Nice to See Your Old

Face Again

'Dig for Victory' was another initiative to get everyone growing food, to boost production from farms and replace imports. Women and children were encouraged to use every spare scrap of land for a vegetable plot and self-sufficiency was not seen as the 'good life', but a necessity.

It Will be Nice to See Your Old Face Again
Valentine's (609)
1942

IT WILL BE NICE TO SEE YOUR OL' FACE AGAIN!

Alone I Did It!

'Alone I Did It!' seems to reflect on the fact that during 1940s Mabel Lucie was a widow working alone in her studio in London, her daughter was busy with family in the country and her son Peter was more musical than artist, he may have helped with the captions and administration, but as with many other women she had to tackle her work alone.

Make a Little Garden

During the war Mabel Lucie worked in her daughter's garden, 'Now leave the garden alone for a bit' her agent added as postscript when he needed new designs and she was busy outside.

Alone I Did It!
Valentine's (868)
1946

Make a Little Garden
Valentine's (562)
1941

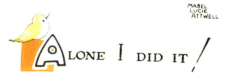

Alone I did it!

Make a little garden –
As gay as it can be, –
A happy little garden
For other folk to see –
A little garden
Which-some day,
May cheer some sad one-
on the way!

Now P'raps you'll Remember Me!

Here's A Four Leaf Clover

Mabel Lucie also acknowledges the therapeutic effect of gardening. She enjoyed the countryside and walking. She uses the flowers as plants to communicate in many of the designs, clover for luck, forget-me-nots and rosemary for remembrance. The garden also features in postcards welcoming people home and helping them recover from the trauma of war.

Now P'raps you'll Remember Me!
Valentine's (490)
1940

Here's A Four Leaf Clover
Valentine's (4584)
1941

NOW P'RAPS YOU'LL REMEMBER ME !

HERE'S A FOUR LEAF CLOVER—
——YOUR TROUBLE'S OVER !

I'd Share My Last Crust with You

When Can We 'Meat' Again?

'When Can We 'Meat' Again?' echoes the words of the three witches in Shakespeare's *Macbeth* as they stirred a cauldron and were thus able to influence the outcome of the battle from behind the scenes.

I'd Share My Last
Crust with You
Valentine's (3858)
1937

When Can We 'Meat'
Again?
Valentine's (393)
1940

I'D SHARE MY LAST CRUST WIF YOU!

WHEN CAN WE "MEAT" AGAIN?

Now What Shall I Give 'em Today?

If I Had Some Onions

Food of all kinds was rationed during the war and Mabel Lucie's postcards reflect the lack of meat in particular. Her father had owned butchers' shops and trade must have been difficult for these types of businesses; people had to queue for their share. They ate more unusual parts of the animals in the form of sausages and meats like chicken, duck and rabbit became more popular as it was possible for you to keep and breed your own. In 1940 Valentine's were keen to have a collection about rationing and there is mention of citrus fruit and onions, but Mabel Lucie bases her response to their request on her own experience.

Now What Shall I Give 'em Today?
Valentine's (808)
1945

If I Had Some Onions
Valentine's (569)
1941

Now — wot shall I give 'em to-day?

IF I had some onions I'd make you a lovely meat pie — — If I had any meat /

A Bit Tied Up Just Now

– But Cheerio!

This comic view of the Blitz is typical of Mabel Lucie's determination to remain cheerful, even in the face of the bombings which plagued London.

A Bit Tied Up Just Now – But Cheerio!
Valentine's (735)
1943

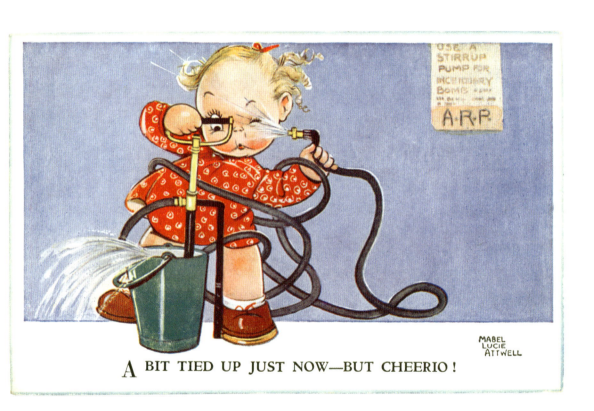

A BIT TIED UP JUST NOW—BUT CHEERIO !

OO! That Feeling

As early as 1935 the government started to prepare for possible air raids. A.R.P. stands for Air Raid Precautions. Mabel Lucie said she did not use shelters but preferred to take her chances and carry on working. Documents from her studio's landlords enforcing new precautions survive amongst her papers and her agents also told her of changes in regulations, such as leaving your offices unlocked. Her postcards show how people stayed up late on fire watch and had to be ready to deal with incendiary devices.

OO! That Feeling
Valentine's (4751)
1939

OO!——THAT FEELING I TAKES TO BED WITH ME——
——WHEN I'VE BEEN DOIN' ME A.R.P.!

Don't Mind the Blackouts

Before We Close our Blackouts

Blackouts feature in several cards in the 1940s, as with the First World War it was vital to keep as dark as possible, so that enemy bombers could not be guided to a target. Skylights were painted black and windows draped in thick curtains. Other lessons were learnt from the first war and everyone was issued with a gas mask in their khaki carry cases, these feature in many of the designs for 1939.

Don't Mind the Blackouts
Valentine's (130)
1939

Before We Close our Blackouts
Valentine's (604)
1942

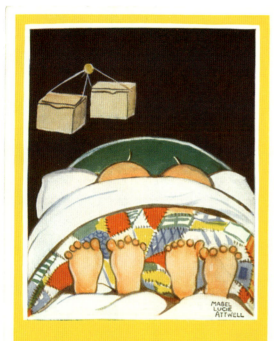

DON'T MIND
THE BLACK-OUTS——
YOU CAN ALWAYS
STAY THE NIGHT!

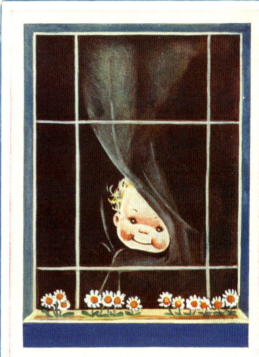

BEFORE WE CLOSE OUR BLACKOUTS
THIS IS WHAT WE'LL DO———
YOU SEND A LOVING THOUGHT TO ME
AN' I'LL SEND ONE TO YOU!

This Courtesy Cops Me

Never Kiss a Girl in a Blackout

'It wasn't the lights I was showing – it was me eyes' – Mabel Lucie liked quality cars and was one of the women to develop a love of driving in the 1920s. Her popular driving card was republished in the war years with a new caption warning about headlights in the blackout. Several times in the descriptions of Mabel Lucie, there is reference to the twinkle in her eyes.

This Courtesy Cops Me
Valentine's
(4244/271)
1938/39

Never Kiss a Girl in a Blackout
Valentine's (213)
1939

Keep It Dark

There were other hazards of the blackout, not just simply
seeing and getting around; one was also kept in the
dark through censorship and secrecy. The Ministry of
Information issued a poster campaign with the strap line
of 'Careless Talk Costs Lives' illustrated by a contemporary
artist with humorous appeal, Fougasse.

Mabel too was playing her part and encouraging secrecy.
Woman worked in intelligence throughout the war. Her
character displays a large corsage in suffragette colours of
green and purple and a fashionable pink gas mask case, a
very modern image of a confident, independent woman.

Keep It Dark
Valentine's (392)
1940

All Up in the Air

Best Make the Best of Things

With rationing and war work it was difficult for women to dress up. Hair was cut short or worn up and tied in scarf so that it was not a hazard at work. So when they had the opportunity they often spent time on their hair and extraordinary little hats.

All Up in the Air
Valentine's (4430)
1939

Best Make the Best of Things
Valentine's (493)
1940

A<small>LL</small> ' <small>UP</small> ' <small>IN THE</small> ' <small>AIR</small>.'

B<small>EST MAKE THE BEST OF THINGS</small>.

It's Stockin's

Say Do I Buy Some More 'Slacks'

Silk stockings and the new nylons were difficult to get hold of and the shorter wartime skirts, put a focus on the legs. Woollen stockings and slacks were necessary for work but women still wanted to look good when they went out.

All accounts show that Mabel Lucie liked to keep up with fashion and socialise at events such as the Arts Club Ball. Women in wartime had to find a way to retain normality and the postcards capture the effort involved.

It's Stockin's
Valentine's (401)
1940

Say Do I Buy Some More 'Slacks'
Valentine's (752)
1944

IT'S STOCKIN'S——WOT'S
MY "BLUE PENCIL" HEADACHE!

SAY! DO I BUY SOME MORE "SLACKS"
TO SAVE WEARING MY STOCKINGS—
OR STOCKINGS—TO SAVE WEARING
MY "SLACKS"?

The Sun is Out

I Loves Me Country

The Sun is Out
Valentine's (876)
1946

I Loves Me Country
Valentine's (734)
1943

Despite the hardships, Mabel Lucie's characters retain their sunny dispositions.

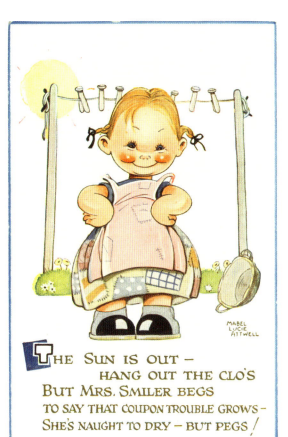

THE SUN IS OUT –
HANG OUT THE CLO'S
BUT MRS. SMILER BEGS
TO SAY THAT COUPON TROUBLE GROWS –
SHE'S NAUGHT TO DRY – BUT PEGS!

I LOVES ME COUNTRY—BUT—CAN'T
GET POWDER—LIPSTICK—PAINT
IT MAKES US LITTLE SMART ONES
LOOK "GOOD"—WOT'S WOT WE AIN'T!

Birthday Greetings Just to Let You See

May All Your Doubles

During the Second World War, Valentine's and Mabel Lucie Attwell reused some of the postcard imagery on calendars with themes such as gardening. She also produced a series of little booklets, not larger than the cards, with titles like 'Comforting Thoughts'. They could be sent as small gifts or in the place of a card, simply to show your support for friends in need. 'Home Fires' was the title given to one card, which was then also made available as a birthday postcard. Both are examples of working around the wartime restrictions. Mabel was certainly keeping the home fires burning whilst the men were away.

Birthday Greetings Just to Let You See
Valentine's (2469)
1933 reprinted

May All Your Doubles
Valentine's (717)
1943

Birthday Greetings JUST TO LET YOU SEE 'TIS TRUE— WE'RE ALL OF US THINKING TO-DAY OF YOU.

MAY ALL YOUR TROUBLES BE CURED BY YOUR "DOUBLES."

Jus' Wishful Thinking!

I'm Fine – How's Yourself?

Jus' Wishful Thinking!
Valentine's (751)
1944

I'm Fine – How's Yourself?
Valentine's (131)
1939

JUS' WISHFUL THINKING!

I'M FINE——HOW'S YOU'SELF!

Cheer-up Everybody

Mabel Lucie has a number of objects or symbols that reappear in lots of these postcards. Some are there to please her Scottish market and others are well-known symbols of good luck. Umbrellas are often open when times are hard and closed when things are better. Although many of the designs do not have backgrounds, she uses the sun and moon to change the mood of the cards, reinforcing the message. John Henty, a collector and expert on her work, noted that she started using black backgrounds only after her own bereavements in the late 1930s.

Cheer-up Everybody
Valentine's (400)
1940

CHEER UP—EVERYBODY—THE JOLLY 'OLE SUN
WILL SHINE AGAIN!

I'm Bringing Good Luck –

Wherever You Are!

Hullo! Hullo!

I'm Bringing Good Luck – Wherever You Are!
Valentine's (132)
1939

Hullo! Hullo!
Valentine's (805)
1945

I'M BRINGING GOOD LUCK—
WHEREVER YOU ARE!

Smiling Even Through the Tears

Today the original artwork of her crying children does not sell in galleries, but in its day it had its purpose and was linked to wartime songs like 'The White Cliffs of Dover'. Well into the 1950s prints of crying children by various artists had a place in the popular print market and were used by charities for fundraising.

Smiling Even Through the Tears
Valentine's (3527)
1936 reprinted

SMILING —
EVEN THROUGH
THE TEARS

Oh Yes – Ours is a Utility Baby!

Auntie's Utility's

The government controlled the supply of goods not only through coupons but also via regulations on what was allowed to be produced. Approved utility clothing and furnishings were designed and made as an alternative to more costly pre-war designs. Mabel Lucie sees humour in the encouragement of production and the effect utility design had on the public. The backs of several of the cards have an additional quotation from the Minster of Production. Mabel seems to be calling wartime and baby boom babies 'utility' babies, certainly couples were being encouraged to marry and have families: '"T.N.T." – To-day Not To-morrow!' The Minister of Production

Oh Yes – Ours is a Utility Baby
Valentine's (756)
1944

Auntie's Utility's
Valentine's (886)
1946

"OH YES——OURS IS
A UTILITY BABY!"

AUNTIE'S UTILITY'S
COME DOWN TO ME!

Oi!

There'll Always *be an England*

Mabel Lucie Attwell remained patriotic throughout the war, with new designs based on music hall songs like 'There'll *Always* be an England' composed by Ross Parker and Hugh Charles in 1939. She also reworked designs like 'Oi!' based on the popular stage show the 'Lambeth Walk', into simple, bold and cheery designs.

Oi!
Valentine's (4429)
1938

There'll Always *be an England*
Valentine's (533)
1941

O I !

"THERE WILL ALWAYS
BE AN ENGLAND!"

Just Won't it be Lov-er-ly

Cheerio!

Towards the end of the war her new artwork echoes official posters of the era, encouraging the public's effort with wartime reconstruction. There are other illustrations that simply looked forward to peace and welcoming loved ones home – the blue birds have come back to roost.

Just Won't it be Lov-er-ly
Valentine's (396)
1940

Cheerio!
Valentine's (1168)
1947

JUST WON'T IT BE LOV-ER-LY—WHEN YOU COME BACK!

Home's a Grand Place to Get

Back To

Home's a Grand Place
to Get Back To
Valentine's (877)
1945

HOME'S A GRAND PLACE
TO GET BACK TO!

FURTHER READING

Adie, Kate, *Corsets to Camouflage Women and War* (London: Hodder and Stoughton/Imperial War Museum, 2003)

Attwell, Mabel Lucie, *Bunty and The Boo-Boos* (series) (London: Raphael Tuck and Sons,1920–22)

Attwell, Mabel Lucie, *Comforting Thoughts* (Dundee: Valentine's, undated)

Babb, Paul and Gay Owen, *Bonzo: the Life and Work of George Study* (Shepton Beauchamp: Richard Dennis, 1988)

Beetles, Chris, *Mabel Lucie Attwell – An Appreciation* (London: Pavilion Press, 1988)

Buckland, Elfreda, *The World Of Donald McGill* (Poole: Blandford Press, 1984)

Buday, George, *The History of the Christmas Card* (London: Spring Books, 1964)

Gosling, Lucinda, *Brushes and Bayonets – Cartoons, Sketches and Paintings of World War One* (Oxford: Osprey, 1988)

Henty, John (recording), *A Lively Life – Remembering the Artist Mabel Lucie Attwell* (Lewes: John Henty, undated)

Henty, John, *The Collectable World of Mabel Lucie Attwell* (Shepton Beauchamp: Richard Dennis, 1999)

Kingsley, Charles (abridged), *The Water Babies* (London: Raphael Tuck & Sons, 1915)

Red Cross (ed.), *The Queen's Book of the Red Cross* (London: Hodder and Stoughton, 1939)

Staff, Frank, *The Picture Postcard and its Origins* (Cambridge: Lutterworth Press, 1966)